Cave Art

Written by Rob Alcraft

Collins

Cave art

Long ago, in the darkness of caves, people made art. They painted wild beasts, shapes and lines.

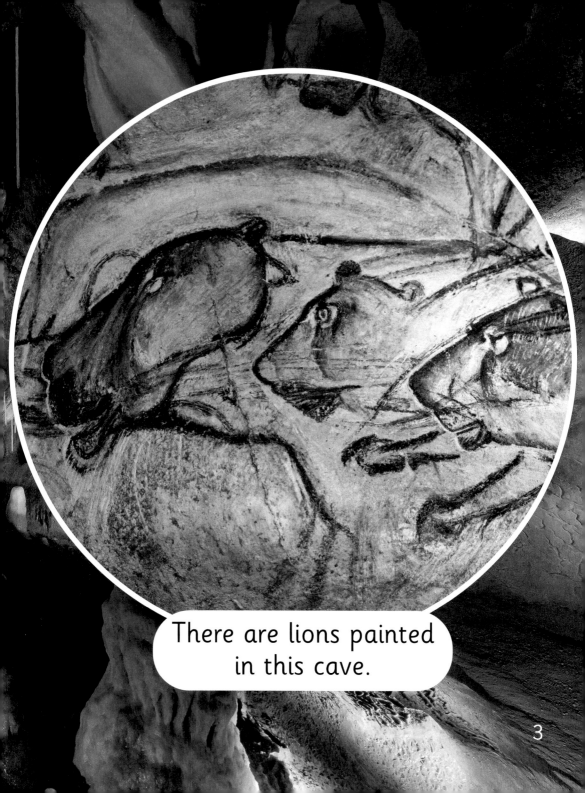

There are lions painted in this cave.

How old?

Cave art was made long ago. Layers of grime show us how old paintings are.

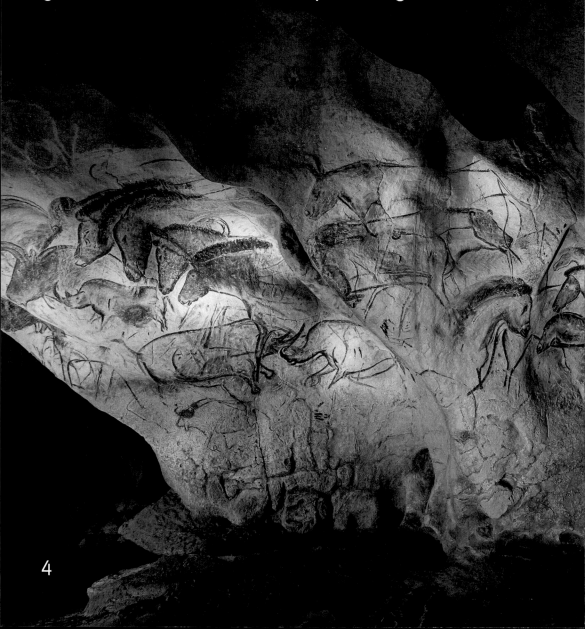

This mammoth was painted over 14,000 years ago.

Global art

People across the globe made cave art.

Handprints show that children painted too.

They made paint by grinding clay and charcoal.

Bold lines

Cave art shows skill. Beasts were painted on the bumps and hollows of the stone.

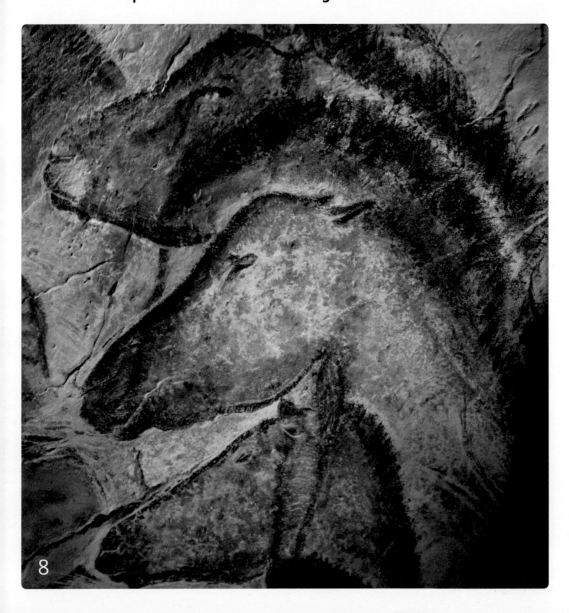

In the shadows, the animals look alive.

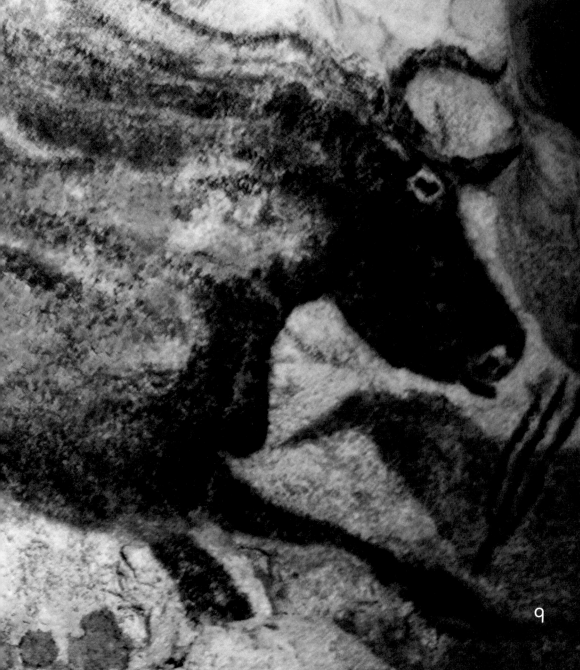

Hollows and ovals

The oldest cave art is shallow hollows and ovals made with stone tools.

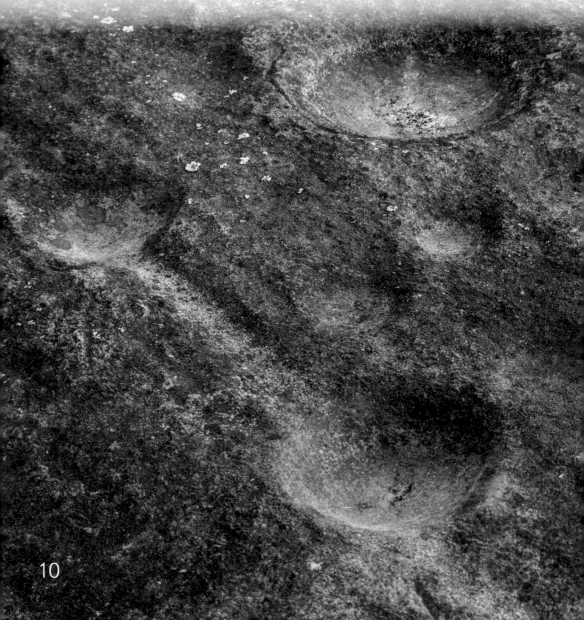

Rows of dots were painted on boulders.

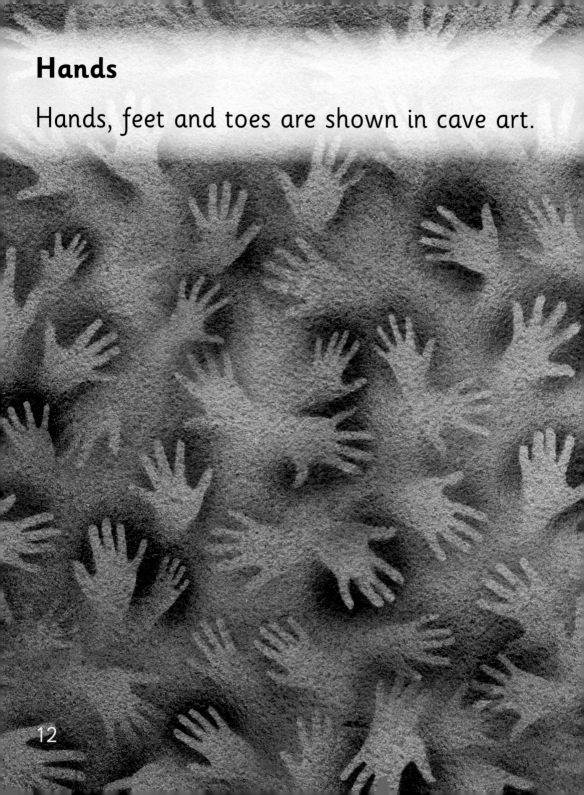

Hands

Hands, feet and toes are shown in cave art.

People made handprints by blowing paint over their hands.

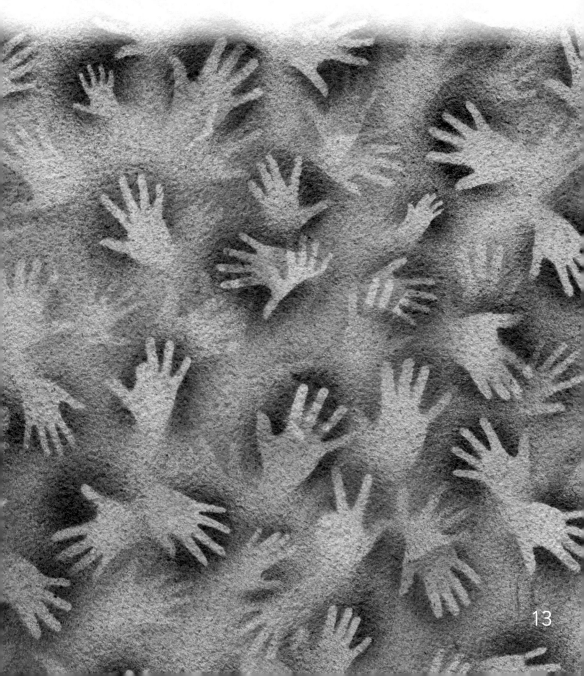

Wild beasts

Some cave art shows wild beasts.
Animals flow across the stone.

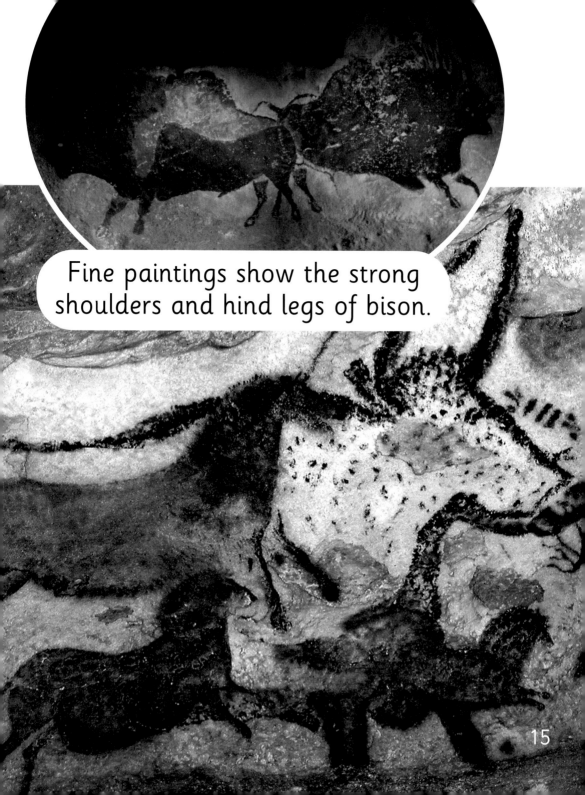

Fine paintings show the strong shoulders and hind legs of bison.

Hunters

Some cave art shows hunting.
Bold hunters throw spears
and hold bows and arrows.
Animals leap away.

This mammoth has been hit with arrows.

Long ago people

Lots of people are shown in cave paintings.

This person holds a snake.

Frozen time

Cave art shows us moments of time, frozen from long ago.

It brings us close to the people that made it.

Make your own cave art

Cave artists painted with black, red, browns and yellows.

hands

wild beasts

lines and dots

23

 After reading

Letters and Sounds: Phase 5

Word count: 249

Focus phonemes: /igh/ i, i-e /ai/ ay, ey, a-e /oa/ o, oe, ow, ou, o-e /ee/ ea

Common exception words: come, into, there, was, some, your, of, to, the, by, are, were, people, their

Curriculum links: Art and design; History

National Curriculum learning objectives: Reading/word reading: read accurately by blending sounds in unfamiliar words containing GPCs that have been taught; read common exception words, noting unusual correspondences between spelling and sound and where these occur in a word; read other words of more than one syllable that contain taught GPCs; Reading/comprehension: understand both the books they can already read accurately and fluently and those they listen to by checking that the text makes sense to them as they read, and correcting inaccurate reading

Developing fluency

- Your child may enjoy hearing you read the book.
- Take turns to read a page. Check that your child pauses at commas and reads with expression.

Phonic practice

- Challenge your child to read these words and identify the spellings of any /oa/ and /igh/ sounds.

  stone   ago   lines   globe   hind   shown

- Can your child find the spelling of /oa/ in these longer words? If it helps with their reading remind them to break the words down into syllables.

  shoul-ders   mo-ments   boul-ders   a-rrows

Extending vocabulary

- Challenge your child to suggest synonyms (word with a similar meaning) for these words. Ask them to check their suggestion works in the context of the page.

  page 4: grime (*dirt, muck*)   page 6: global (*worldwide, universal*)

  page 10: hollows (*dips, depressions*)   page 20: frozen (*preserved, kept*)